WEATHER

SUN
AND US

Jillian Powell

Illustrated by Joan Corlass

 Belitha Press

First published in the UK in 1998 by
Belitha Press Limited,
London House, Great Eastern Wharf,
Parkgate Road, London SW11 4NQ

This edition first published in 1999

Text by Jillian Powell
Illustrations by Joan Corlass
Copyright in this format © Belitha Press Limited 1998

Editor Claire Edwards
Series designer Hayley Cove
Picture researcher Diana Morris
Consultants Elizabeth Atkinson & Liz Lewis

ISBN 1 85561 720 X (hardback)
ISBN 1 84138 037 7 (paperback)
ISBN 1 84138 031 8 (Big Book)

Printed in Hong Kong

British Library Cataloguing in Publication Data
for this book is available from the British Library.

9 8 7 6 5 4 3 2 1

Picture acknowledgements
Axiom: 24 Chris Bradley.
Eye Ubiquitous: 22 David Cummings.
Werner Forman Archive: 28 Biblioteca
Universitaria, Bologna.
Getty Images: front cover John Riley, 4 Tim Brown,
6 Jean-Paul Manceau, 10 Terry Vine, 14 Frank Orel,
18 Andy Sacks, 20 Mervyn Rees, 26.
Spectrum Colour Library: 8.
Zefa: 12 & 16 Stockmarket.

Contents

Words in **bold** are explained
on pages 30 and 31.

What is the sun?

The sun is a star.
It is shining far out
in space, 150 million
kilometres away.

The sun is more than a
million times bigger than
the earth. It seems smaller
because it is so far away.

SUN FACT

The earth
travels round
the sun. It takes
just over one year
to go right round.

The sun looks brighter than other stars because it is closer to the earth than they are.

The sun is **billions** of years old. The sun that shone on the dinosaurs is the same one that shines on us today.

The sun's **rays** give us light and warmth. We call its light daylight.

We can only see the sun during the day. Everything on the earth needs sunshine to live and to grow.

Day and night

We call the start of the day **sunrise** and the end of the day **sunset**. The sky is often a lovely colour at these times.

6

SUN FACT

The light from the sun makes the moon shine.

Did you know the sun is shining all the time, even at night when you can't see it?

When we have night, the sun is shining on the other side of the world.

This is because the earth is spinning as it travels round the sun.

On the side of the earth facing the sun it is daytime. On the side facing away, the earth is in darkness and it is night.

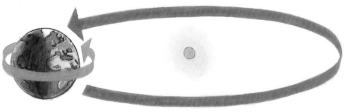

The earth spins round once every 24 hours.

Summer and winter sun

How sunny and hot it is depends on where we live and what **season** it is.

When it is winter in the northern half of the world, it is summer in the southern half. The Australians have Christmas in the summer sun.

SUN FACT

Near the **Equator**, around the middle of the earth, it is hot and sunny all year round.

In summer the sun feels warm and the days are long. The sun is high in the sky and shines strongly. This is because our part of the world is tilted towards the sun.

In winter our part of the world is tilted away from the sun, and the sun is low in the sky. It can still shine brightly, but its **rays** are weak and the air feels cold.

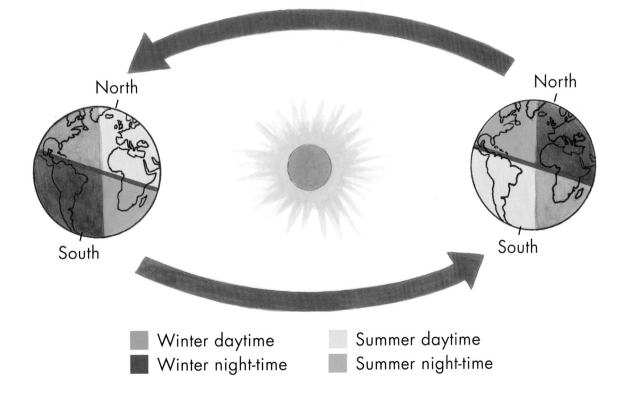

North

South

North

South

Winter daytime

Winter night-time

Summer daytime

Summer night-time

Shadows and rainbows

Shadows are made because the sun's light cannot pass through solid objects. The dark area where the light cannot reach is a shadow.

SUN FACT

You can never reach the end of a rainbow.

At **dawn**, shadows are long. As the earth turns, the sun seems to rise and the shadows grow shorter.

Shadows are shortest when the sun is at its highest point in the sky.

As the sun goes down in the afternoon they grow long again.

Sunlight is made up of lots of colours.

When it is sunny and rainy at the same time, raindrops break sunlight into all its colours and a rainbow appears.

Enjoying the sun

Sunshine can make us feel happy and give us **energy**. On sunny days we can enjoy being out of doors in the fresh air.

Sunlight helps our bodies make **vitamin** D, which keeps our bones and teeth strong and helps our nails grow.

SUN FACT

We smile more on sunny days than on dull days.

The sun's heat makes us thirsty. When we are hot we lose water from our bodies by **sweating**. You can keep cool in the **shade**.

Cold drinks, ice lollies and fruit help us put back water we have lost and keep us cool.

Staying safe in the sun

We need to take care in the sun. Its **rays** can burn our skin and hurt our eyes. Too much sun can make us sick and give us headaches.

Sunshine makes our skin darker. We call this a suntan. It is the skin's way of trying not to burn.

SUN FACT

Pale skin burns more easily than dark skin.

Light-coloured
cotton clothes
feel coolest.

Sunglasses protect
our eyes. Even
with sunglasses
on, never look
straight at the sun.

Sun cream helps to stop
the sun burning us.
We should cover up with
T-shirts and sun hats too.

Sun, plants and animals

Plants trap sunlight in their green leaves. The sunlight helps them make food using water from the soil and **carbon dioxide** from the air. This is called photosynthesis.

SUN FACT

Some plants, such as sunflowers, turn their heads towards the sun.

16

Many flowers, such as dandelions and daisies, open their petals during the day when the sun is shining. They close them at night.

Some birds and animals **sunbathe**. Sunlight helps birds to keep their feathers clean and healthy.

Reptiles need sunshine to warm their blood and give them **energy**.

Harvest and drought

Sunshine **ripens** food **crops**. Wheat and barley turn golden when they are ready to **harvest**. The sun helps to make fruit sweet and good to eat.

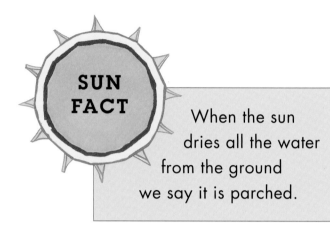

SUN FACT

When the sun dries all the water from the ground we say it is parched.

Some plants need
lots of sunshine and
warmth to ripen.
These plants grow
only in hot countries.

Plants need more
water when it is
hot and sunny.
Farmers must
water their
crops if it
doesn't rain.

When there is no
rain for a long time,
there is a **drought**.

Hot sunshine dries
the soil very quickly.
If there is no water
on the land, plants
and animals will die.

Cities in the sun

In sunny weather cities feel warmer than the countryside. The sun's **rays** heat roads and buildings, which warm the air around them. Buildings trap the sun's heat.

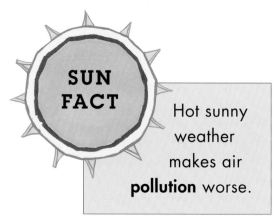

SUN FACT

Hot sunny weather makes air **pollution** worse.

Some offices have air conditioning, which sucks in hot air and blows out cool air. Dark glass windows and **blinds** help to keep out the sun's **rays**.

In hot weather, **fumes** from cars and factories mix with the warm air and make it difficult to breathe.

Parks have trees that give **shade** in the city. Ponds and fountains cool the air around them.

Living in hot countries

In hot countries, houses are built with thick walls to keep out the sun's heat. **Shutters** and **blinds** cover the windows.

SUN FACT

Some of the world's hottest countries also have a lot of rain.

27

CALLE
SEVERO CATALINA

People often wear long, loose clothes to keep cool. They cover their heads to keep off the sun.

Many people take a rest or **siesta** during the hottest part of the day, when the sun is high in the sky.

Hot deserts

In places where there is very little rain, the land is **desert**. Most deserts are very hot during the day.

Some animals and plants have **adapted** to living in deserts. Camels can live for months without water.

SUN FACT

The Sahara Desert in Africa is the sunniest place in the world.

Date palms grow roots that reach deep underground to find water.

The fennec fox has big ears that help it lose heat and stay cool.

Cactus plants can grow in deserts because they store water in their thick **stems**. Some desert animals **burrow** into the sand or hide under rocks during the day. They come out at night when it is cooler.

Sun power

Energy from the sun is called solar energy. **Solar power** stations trap the sun's **rays** on giant mirrors. They heat water boilers to make **steam**, which is used to make electricity.

SUN FACT

In hot countries people use the sun's rays to get salt from the sea.

26

Some houses and cars have **solar panels** on the roof. These make electricity to light and heat houses, and to power cars. Solar energy does not make **pollution**.

People have always used the sun's power to help them. Its heat can dry and burn. It dries grapes into sultanas and raisins, and grass into **hay**.

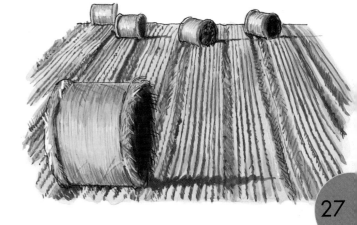

Cocoa beans are spread out on banana leaves to dry in the sun. When they have dried they are used to make chocolate.

Sun worship

In the past many people thought the sun was a powerful god who brought light and heat and **ripened** their **crops**.

The **Aztec** sun god was called Huitzilopochtli. They drew pictures of him, like the one below.

They believed he fought with darkness every night so he could rise again the next morning.

SUN FACT

The **Ancient Egyptians** believed their kings were the sons of the sun god.

In spring, the **Celts** rolled wheels of fire downhill to help give the sun strength.

The Ancient Egyptians believed that their sun god, Re, sailed across the sky every day in a boat.

People built **temples**, like this one at Stonehenge, to show where the sun rose and set at midsummer and midwinter.

Words to remember

adapt To get used to a new place or way of doing something.

Ancient Egyptians People who lived in Egypt more than two thousand years ago.

Aztecs People who lived in Mexico more than five hundred years ago.

billion A billion is a thousand million. Dinosaurs lived on earth 225 million years ago.

blinds Pieces of material or plastic that fit over windows to keep out the sun.

burrow To dig under the ground.

carbon dioxide An invisible gas found in the air.

Celts People who lived in England, Spain and other parts of Europe in Ancient times, before the Romans.

crops Food grown on the land, such as cereals, fruit and vegetables.

dawn First light at the beginning of the day.

desert A dry place where very little can live or grow.

drought Something that happens when there is no rain for a long time, and the land is very dry.

energy Power to make things move. Energy gives us strength to do things.

Equator An imaginary line around the centre of the earth.

fumes Poisonous smoke.

harvest To gather ripe crops.

hay Dried grass that is fed to cows and horses.

pollution Dirt made by people and machines that harms the earth.

rays Thin lines, or beams, of light and heat.

reptiles Creatures with cold blood and scaly skin.

ripen To become ready to eat.

season Part of the year. Each year has four seasons: spring, summer, autumn and winter. Some parts of the world only have two seasons: wet and dry.

shade A place away from the light and heat of the sun.

shutters Wooden doors that shut over windows to keep out the sunlight.

siesta An early afternoon sleep or rest.

solar panels Flat surfaces that draw in energy from the sun.

solar power Power made by the sun's rays. It can be used to heat buildings and pools, and even run cars.

steam The hot white cloud that comes up from boiling water.

stem The part of a plant that holds up the leaves, thorns and flowers.

sunbathe To lie in the sun.

sunrise When the sun rises at the beginning of the day.

sunset When the sun goes down at the end of the day.

sweating Losing water through skin. Sweat helps to cool us down.

temples Buildings where people pray and worship.

vitamins Goodness, found in our food, which we need to keep us healthy.

Index